The Soul Unlimited

Poetry for the Soul

The Soul Unlimited

Poetry for the Soul

DAVID A. JORDAN

WESTBOW
PRESS
A DIVISION OF THOMAS NELSON

WestBow Press books may be ordered through booksellers or by contacting:

WestBow Press
A Division of Thomas Nelson
1663 Liberty Drive
Bloomington, IN 47403
www.westbowpress.com
1-(866) 928-1240

Because of the dynamic nature of the Internet, any web addresses or links contained in this book may have changed since publication and may no longer be valid. The views expressed in this work are solely those of the author and do not necessarily reflect the views of the publisher, and the publisher hereby disclaims any responsibility for them.

Any people depicted in stock imagery provided by Thinkstock are models, and such images are being used for illustrative purposes only.

Certain stock imagery © Thinkstock.

ISBN: 978-1-4497-6651-1 (sc)
ISBN: 978-1-4497-6649-8 (e)
ISBN: 978-1-4497-6650-4 (hc)

Library of Congress Control Number: 2012916358

Printed in the United States of America

WestBow Press rev. date: 9/4/2012

No Time

I'm out of time.
Time to go,
Go away from here—
Anywhere. It doesn't matter;
There's no time.

I want to run;
I want to hide.
Too late for that;
I blow up.
I'm out of time.

Death runs and taps my shoulder
And takes my soul.
I have no spirit.
I'm out of time.

Fate sprints and takes my lifeline.
It cut it fast and quick.
I reach the spirit realm;
No one can guide me.

There's no time.

Who Am I?

I define myself as a beautiful person.
People don't define me by the way they act
But by themselves,
I am me unto me.

I'm courteous and show love to my enemies;
I take the hatred in and turn it out as love
To show others who they are.

Who am I? Am I a goddess or a king?
Do you define me as ugly or beautiful?
God is the one who defines me
As a true person to love and be loved.

God defines me as a true person in his eyes,
One that shows the human race that
He is the one, true God.
He is the one who loved us,
Created us, and made us in his image.

That's who I am,
Yes. That's the true,
Divine *me.*

Today's Youth

The youth of today are the youth of tomorrow.
We are the kids of the future;
Yes.
That is who we are,
Don't you think?

We are special.
We don't have to work in a place
That isn't good enough.

Look how far we have come:
Obama is now president.
If he can do it,
So can we.

Just like Obama's motto, *Yes, we can,*
We can if we just believe.
All the opportunities we have—
Let's use them.
We can be great.

I am proud to be alive.
I know you are;
I know we can make it.
I know who we are.
We are *kids of the future!*

Being Black is Bold

Being black is bold.
Black is the color we are;
Bold is how we treat the world.
Look and see all we have come through.

Why
Is a question we ask.
Why do we treat each other the way we do?
Why can't we go back to the way we used to be?

One family,
One community.
People didn't know each other but acted as if they did.
They were faithful but truthful with one another.

If we made it through slavery and
Segregation, then we can make it through this time.

Being black is bold.
Look at what we have:
Black love,
Black power,
And the ability to be black.

We made it through, even though they thought we were
nothing
We are something
We are black!

Sunset Hills

The sun is setting, and so am I.
When I die, the sun will rise another day, and I will be in
heaven someday.
Although I will be gone, don't wait for me
Or try to bring me back.
I will be at the throne of God.

I trust you to trust me.
But this life is gone, so don't trust
Anyone but God.
My love for him is strong;
My passion to share his daily bread
Is also strong.

My brethren, be strong.
Now is the time of need.
In these last and evil days,
Sunset hills are near and far,
For my time to go is now.

I hope you will be strong.
The hour of your destiny is near.
Take God's Word to heart;
He will always show you the way.
He is here now and forever;
Trust in him always.

The Power of Love

Love is the trust
We depend upon.
Love is the life
In others and ourselves.

L is for living people to love us.
O is for the options love gives us.
V is for the very God who loves us.
E is for everyone
And everybody to love
And be loved.

Love is friendship.
Fear is in love;
We fear God,
And he loves us.

The power of love is life
Inside ourselves.

A part of ourselves
Is love.

That Kiss

That kiss
> Held my whole world;
> I wanted to have it
> Over and over again—
> That kiss.

That kiss
> Was so beautiful,
> No other kiss compared.
> My lips never found lips so
> Divine, so perfect—
> That kiss.

That kiss
> Made me stop and think,
> Did I really want this?
> Did I want you?
> Would you be mine?
> That was all I thought—
> That kiss.

That kiss
> Made my head spin.
> It made me so dizzy
> I grabbed you.
> More, I wanted more
> Of you—
That kiss.

A

A perfect love,
A stolen heart,
A love so passionate,
A deep understanding,
A beautiful soul.

The letter A can make my day.

Can You Be Mine?

In my head, I asked them,
Can you be mine?
Can you love me how I want you to?

In my head I asked them,
Will you make my dreams
Realities?
Will you love me for myself?

In my head I asked them
Question after
Question after question.

Your Smile

Your smile
Matches mine.

Your smile
Makes me a little happier
Every time I see you.

Your eyes
Make mine want to gaze into yours.

Your body
Makes me want to
Explore all its wonders.

Your lips
Make me wonder how it would feel
To be kissed
By those beautiful lips.

Your hand
Makes me want to grab it.
How would it feel to hold your hand in mine?

All of this came from your beautiful,
Warm, loving smile.

I Want, but I Can't Have

I want them,
But I can't have them.

I want to kiss them,
But I can't have their lips.

I want to hold them in my arms,
But I can't have them.

I want to look into their eyes
And for them to look in mine,
But I can't have their attention.

I want to hold their hands,
But they're not mine to hold.

I want to have their heads
Lay on my chest,
But those heads will never
Be mine.

I want them,
But I can't have them.

Color Doesn't Matter

You can be
Black—
Black as night—
But I'll still love you.

You can be
White—
White as the snow on the ground—
But I'll still love you.

You can be
Green—
Green as the grass—
But I'll still love you.

You can be
Red—
Red as the blood that
Flows through your veins—
But I'll still love you.

No matter your color,
No matter your face,
Color doesn't matter.

Someone to Catch my Falling Heart

My heart is falling,
Falling toward the dirty floor.
The dirty floor is rising,
Rising to meet my heart.

My heart is tumbling,
Tumbling down the hill of loneliness.
The hill of loneliness is growing,
Growing to make my fall longer.

I fall longer, so does my weeping.
My weeping heart cries for a hand,
A hand to catch me, and then I stop.
I stop falling, and I'm in shock.

Shocked that someone caught me,
Caught me and my falling heart.
My falling heart was held in human hands.
In human hands, my heart's tears were dried away.

My tears dried up,
Dried up into the air.
The air will hold them until I fall again.
I won't fall again;
Someone caught my falling heart.

You Blushed.

You blushed
 When I looked into your eyes.

You blushed
 When I kissed you.

You blushed
 When I held you close and told you I loved you.

You blushed.
You blushed.
You blushed.

River

Running water,
Flowing smoothly over the rocks,
Rolling gently under bridges and
The fallen trees of old times.

Holding a story—
The stories of past and present,
The fight over land
Between the animals that run wild and the
People who want to own something that's not
Theirs to own.

Made small,
Pushed toward a constant flow,
It gets angry at the people
Who put their mass destruction in its path.

Ruined,
Filled with the waste of man,
Running roughly over rocks,
Killing nature in its path.

Dry,
No more water to flow.
Gone because of carelessness,
It can come back,
But it doesn't have to go.

You can save it.
Will you save the river?

A Letter from God

My child,

I am grateful you are of mine. Heaven rejoiced
When you received my son as your savior.
When things are rough, you may call on me,
Ask for my advice. Take my hand, and I will
Guide you. I will carry you through your
Hardships. Keep your head held high and do all
Things in my glory. My light will shine
Through you—just put forth the effort and
Release my word, my power, and my love. You are a Christian,
a follower of my son Jesus Christ.
I love you when you worship me and
When you struggle in your hardships. I am the
Rock you stand upon. I am your father.
We will see each other in heaven.

Love Your Father
God

Trees

I stand tall,
Tall and proud.
I give you a life,
Yet you cut me down.

You destroy me;
I am a home for other creatures.
You destroy their homes.

You turn me into the
Something less than what I am

We will be no more.

None of us stands tall.
There's none of us to be proud;
Mankind is extinct.

But you can save me;
You can save us.

I will stand tall;
I will live on.

I am a tree.

Just You

Your eyes,
      Your smile
Put me on edge
Every time I see you.

Your laugh,
      Your voice
Make me squirm
Whenever you're near.

Your face,
      Your body
That has me dreaming of you
And wishing you were mine.

I want to look into your eyes with deep passion, and I want to
kiss you.

I want to look at your smile when I'm hugging you
And smile to match yours.

Maybe your laugh sounds so sweet
And perfect that I have to join in.

Just your voice, that anybody will listen to,
But I just want to hear you next to me.

Yes, just you,
Sitting next to me,
Laying next to me,
Kissing me,
Holding me in your arms.

Just you.

A Family

Our ups and our downs—
The way we love each other.
We work together to help one another.

A family:
As one person,
A group that loves, cherishes,
And keeps one another.

A community:
As one body,
A body working together
To get a job done.

We are one people.

No matter the color of our skin,
No matter the different
Worlds we come from.

No matter the people that talk about us,
We are a family.

Save Me

I slowly die;
You're destroying me.
Keep me alive.

Save me.

I'm withering in pain;
You're killing me.
Keep me.

Heal me,
Save me.

I am Earth.

I will not live forever.

Save me,
Save me.

Mother Earth.

Nervous

Nervous—
When you leaned in for a kiss,
What if I hadn't done it right?
Would you laugh at me?
Or dump me?

Nervous—
On our first date,
What if I'd said something wrong?
Or was too pushy?

Nervous—
The first time we held hands,
Was mine too sweaty,
Too cold,
Or just right?

Nervous—
When you asked me out,
How would you have felt if I'd said no?
Or what if you had changed your mind
About me?

Nervous—
When you say you love me,
Should I say it back?

Nervousness dispatches with love—
It's a feeling we get
When we're out of love.

I'm not nervous anymore;
I guess you changed that.

Subway

Loud,
I can't think,
Speeding between stops,
No one talking.
But I write,
A place of relaxation,
No one to bother me
Or my imagination.
It never jumps outside the doors but it stays
Closed inside,
My subway escape.

Omnipresence

Always there, never away,
Standing right next to me,
Catching me when I fall,
Lifting me back up on my feet.

Carrying me through my hardships,
Holding me in your arms,
When the path seems narrow
And I feel I can't make it.

Moving with me as the wind pushes me,
And holding my parents' hands
As their lives move on
As well as mine.

Never failing or falling,
There when I shed my tears,
And there when I'm overjoyed,
Rejoicing in your name.

Your omnipresence never fails:
Here always.
Your son saved me.

The Holy Spirit comforts me.

You advise me as my father;
Your omnipresence comforts me.

Fell from Heaven

A blessing,
A life.
Your son
Fell from heaven.

To save me,
To hold me in your arms.
But you
Never fell from heaven.

But you help me,
Even if I can't see you.
But I believe in you;
Your love falls from heaven.

Your words,
Your power,
Fell from heaven.

You

You held me in your arms;
I held you in mine.
I felt calm in your presence;
Just the feeling of your nearness
Slowed time down.

You smiled at me
When I was scared to talk to you.
You talked to me and you complimented me.

You asked me out when I
Didn't know what to do.
You kissed me softly;
That proved you liked me for me.

You are mine,
And I am yours.
You give me a reason to
Be myself and not be ashamed.

A White Rose

A single flower,
The color of life,
Standing alone,
Given out of love.

Most beautiful flower,
A flower of loyalty,
Loyalty of love,
From one to another.

A symbol of one's love,
Of one's affection,
To show a person's true
Feelings of love.

It doesn't have to be
Put in a bunch,
But a single flower,
A single love.

A love like no other,
A symbol like no other.

A white rose.

Our Love

Your eyes,
> That are as beautiful
> As the moon's light,
> The great blue ocean.

Your smile,
> That shines as bright
> As the sun on a
> Fall afternoon.

Your lips,
> That yearn for a kiss,
> Their softness as soft as silk
> But as firm as steel.

Your heart,
> As steady as an African beat,
> A rhythm so powerful
> And so meant to be.

Our love,
> A stronger bond than the
> Particles of steel itself,
> We stay together.

You and me,
> Me and you.

Our love

Escape

Behind a door,
In a room,
Locked away,
Never to be seen again.

Yet the door creaked open;
It walked out of the room,
Broke open the lock,
And it was seen.

An animal that
Could rip your life apart
Would kill your very soul,
And you'd never be the same.

Your world comes crashing down.
It seems everyone's against you—
Cold and dark,
Bumps of embarrassment,

Caused by the door's opening.
But good comes out;
You are free.
The weight's off your chest.

Soaring above all others,
Winning at all you do,
Showing the world *you.*

Now,
Outside the door,
In the open,
For all to see
       Me!

Rescue Me

Rescue me
From my sorrow,
From my pain,
From my forbidden love.

Rescue me
From my doubt,
From my dark love,
From behind my wall of shame.

Rescue my
Burning heart,
Aching for love,
Burning deep into my soul.

Rescue my
Newfound love
And help me
Love.

Rescue me
And sweep me off my feet;
Carry me off
And away into the sunset.

Rescue me;
Save me.

Upward

Used to
Tears falling
Down,
Leaving you with no hope.

What if they went up?
With a dream inside
Or maybe a thought?

Went up with hope,
And hope is what
Fueled them.

Up toward the heavens,
Crying out to be made
Free and wanting to be
Free.

It never rained down
On your head.
Hope made it rain up,
Made your tears travel.

Happy they found hope,
Hope to be real,
A real dream,
A real thought.

They went up.

Will

The will of man
Is nothing
But a small pull at your flesh,
At your mind.

Destroyed by man's
Weapons,
By the words and the
Physical displacement
Of man.

But the power of God
Is extraordinary.
It is the force of nature—
Your conscience.

Nothing can destroy his
Power. Hi power is like a nuclear bomb
And it's Dropped on a person of strong
Faith.

If he and God are of one,
God's will flows
Through his veins.

By the power of God, that
Bomb can be stopped
Or move a mountain.

Don't get confused
By your fleshly desires,
But bring forth the
Power of God.

A Blue Butterfly

It flew away.
It flew to the heavens;
It was her spirit,
A blue butterfly.

She breathed her last breath;
She looked at peace;
She closed her eyes
And went on to glory.

She flew and flew
Over the old world she knew.
We saw after she left
Her spirit was a blue butterfly.

She never cried;
Heaven rejoiced when she arrived.
I looked out in the blue sky and saw
A pretty blue butterfly.

Memories of her flooded me;
I closed my eyes and saw her one last time.
She was flying through the sky,
Watching her family
As a blue butterfly.

Even after the rain,
When the sun came out,
When the rainbow shined through the sky,
The last time I saw her,
She was a blue butterfly.

Her butterfly flew over me;
I saw her in my mind.

I watched her butterfly fly away
And fade into the sky.

That was the last time I saw her blue butterfly.

Final Act

This act is ending;
The curtains are closing.
What's the finale, you ask?
God's coming back.

The rapture is his ending.
It picks up in part two:
New heaven and new earth.

No more pain,
No more suffering,
No more sorrow,
No more sin.

We will walk through
Heaven's gates with
Our gift in hand:
Eternal life.

With God and his Son,
Forever more,
We will walk the streets
Paved *with gold.*

A house of our own.
We'll see loved ones;
We'll see sin no more.

That's the final act,
But hold your applause.
It's not over yet.

Hope

A star in the sky,
Its light twinkling bright,
Gave us hope.

A flower in weeds,
Something beautiful
In all doubt and wrong.

Rain falling
In the summer heat,
Cooling the ground.

Hopeful for a baby's
Cry after their born.

Hope for a God
Greater than a world itself.

Not a person,
But a spirit
Being you can rely on.

Hope for a happiness over
People's believing that
good will happen.

Hope.

If Love Could Die

If love could die,
So would I.
My heart would shatter,
And my soul would crumble.

If love could die,
I wouldn't be able to stand.
My legs would grow weak,
And I wouldn't be able to walk.

If love could die,
My voice wouldn't be heard.
It would die away
With the rushing wind.

If love could die,
So would my family:
No mother to hold me,
No father to scold me.

If love could die,
The world would burn
With all of us in
Mother Nature's wrath.

But love can't die;
My soul lives on,
And my heart is saved.
Love can't die <3.

Havoc

Hatred and anger
Fuel me,
Make my eyes
Flash with anger.

But at some point,
There are still
Waters inside me.
The ocean is calm.

Then it quakes,
And a tsunami
Rages over my
Still waters.

A cold front
Meets the warm,
Still waters
And is grabbed by
The tsunami.

And it hits land
Destroying everything;
Its rage stops
At nothing.

My job is still not done.
I look at the havoc
I created and smile
My sinister smile.

The job is almost done,
But I realize I let
The tsunami flow
Out of my mouth.

Instead, I talk,
I write
About my anger,
My hatred.

There would be no
Damage to the
Ones I hold close,
The ones I love.

Rewind

Hatred and anger
No longer fuel me.
My eyes flash with
Happiness.

There's no quake,
No hurricane.

I am still;
I am happy.

The darkness is gone
From my soul.

No End

In space,
A line.
It has have no end.

From our galaxy
To another,
Past Pluto,
Beyond the Oort Cloud,

There's infinity,
Far away.

When we think we're closer,
It seems farther away.

It's never close enough
That I can touch it
But always far away.

I follow it;
I keep going.

I grow old;
I've wasted my life.

One question comes to mind:

What was I looking for?
I close my eyes.

Find You

Through time,
Through space,
I will find you.

Across the sea,
Over the mountains,
Through the deserts,
I will find you.

The first step
I take
Through Mother Nature.

The first step
Of my journey,
And I can't see
Where I am going.

Eventually, I see you:
My finish line.
I will cross.

A long way
To heart,
But I will find it.
I will find you;
I'll hold you close,
Never let you go.
I found you.

See

I see
Into your eyes,
Into your soul.

I see
Your passion,
Your affection.

I see
Beyond your appearance,
Your personality.

I see
You every night,
And every time
I close my eyes.

Every night
I lay down
To sleep

And hope the
Next time
I'll be with you.

I see you.

To Love

Under the sea,
Whales cry
For one another.

In the trees,
The birds sing
For one another.

We look
Into each
Other's eyes,

And we know
From that look
That we belong to each other.

We know we'll
Love each other
For who we are.

We won't be
Scared to show
Our affection (even in public).

One land,
We yearn
For another soul
To love.

If Hate …

If hate fueled us, the
World wouldn't be the same.

Blood would be shed,
Man would kill anyone who
Did not resemble him.

The ground would be stained
With the blood of our mothers and fathers.

The rivers would flow red with the blood
Of our brothers and sisters.

The Red Sea would live up to
Its dreaded name.

If hate didn't fuel us, the world
Would be in peace.

Blood may be shed, but only
For desperate measures.

The ground would stay green and the soil
Fertile. Our mothers and fathers would live
To teach us right from wrong.

The rivers would run water and fish or be as muddy
As the mighty Amazon River.

Hate doesn't fuel me; don't let it fuel you.
Love instead of hate.

Love your enemies, your friends, and family.

Don't hate.

The One I Love

There's a stronger force
Pulling me
Toward the one I love.

There's music,
Love's call
To me.

I know
There's a map
Pointing to my true love.

There's a soul just
For me;
I can feel it.

There's a brighter
Twinkle in my eye
Every time I see

The one I love.

My Eyes

Behind my eyes,
There's a moment
In time
When I dream of love.

Behind my eyes,
There's a passion
That loves
Only one person.

In front of my eyes,
There's a moment
In time
Where love is real.

In front of my eyes,
There's a passion
That is
For one person.

In front of my eyes,
Everyone
Is kind,
No matter who you are.

Life

L: Living despite the obstacles in life,
  Surviving downfalls
  And grief,
  Living through the deepest, darkest
  Moments.

I: Integrity gained through age,
  And wisdom to teach those
  Younger than ourselves,
  Because we've all inhabited
  Younger natures.

F: Fulfillment, we have conquered.
  We have found our purpose,
  Our way to save a dying generation,
  To live and show the world the true me.

E: Expectation for a younger one to do better
  Than ourselves; experience, for we
  Have enjoyed our youth, enjoyed
  Our life.

We grow old and smile
At life's old memories.
We laugh at moments past.

Life, a living flower,
Beautiful, but it must
Die too.

Life.

Out of Love

I've fallen in and out of love and
Never found the right one.
I looked high and low but
Still can't find love.

Looking for a lover,
Looking for love,
Searching throughout my life
For the right one.

Out there somewhere
Is my love.
Out in the world is
The right person, just for me.

Valiant and proud,
We'll never downsize
Our love for each other.

Enchanted and magical,
Our love will always
Have a spark.

We'll always love each other,
Not for appearances but
For our personalities,
Our passions.

Love—
I couldn't seem to find it,
But it found me.
I hold love to my heart.
Love.

Understand

No one truly
Understands
What goes on
In my heart,
In my head.

If they truly
Knew what I
Thought, what I
Felt, despite
The discrimination,

If they knew,
Would they
Call me the names
They do?

Would they understand
The hell I've been
Through; the nonstop
Hate pushed like a knife
Into my heart?

Would I be able to walk
With my head up, no matter
What people say
Or how they look at me?

One truly
Understands
What goes on
In my heart,
In my head.

One person truly
Knows what I
Think, how I
Feel, despite
Discrimination.

One person knows
And she doesn't
Call me the names
Others do.

She understands
The hell I've been
Through; the nonstop
Hate pushed like a knife
Into my heart.

I am able to walk
With my head up, no matter
What people say
Or how they look at me.

Why?

Why are people constantly hurting me?
They don't understand my grief,
My pain, and suffering.

Why do you claim to love me?
You prove to me you don't;
You don't want to be seen with me
And deny me at all costs.

Why is there a hole in my heart?
It can never be filled.
We love and love again,
But love is never there.

Why don't people understand
The hell I go through,
The emotion that
Hacks at my heart?

What people don't see
Are the tears running down
My face,
The heartache.

Why can't they see me
Through my eyes?
Then they could truly
Understand me.

Walk a mile in my shoes,
Then ask
Why?

Always There

Always there
Next to me,
Near where I'm standing.

Always there,
And I fear
I'll say something
I'll regret.

Always there,
So close to me.
I imagine
Holding you in my arms.

Always there
To make me smile,
You know exactly
What to say.

Always there,
But you're
Never mine.

Always there,
But I want you here;
I want you mine.

A Heart

A symbol of
Love and passion,

A heart beats to
Love and understand.

A heart listens to a voice
That cries for help.

A heart loves the
Inside of a person.

A heart lives and loves;
A heart dies, but its love
Never does.

A Baby

I am young.
I don't know
What racism is
Or what hate means.

I don't know that
Guns hurt
Just as much
As words.

I don't know
That there are
People out there
Who wish to hurt me.

I do know
How to give a hug,
Even though I don't
Know how to walk.

I do know
How to love,
And that will
Always
Be a part of me.

In Truth

In truth,
I love you,
But I am too
Scared to tell you.

In truth,
I want to touch
You and feel your
Skin touching mine.

In truth,
I want to
Hold you close
And listen to your heart.

In truth,
My lips have
Never been kissed,
And I want yours on mine.

In truth,
I can't stop
Thinking about you.
I can't get the thought of you out of my head.

In truth,
I love you.
I love your smile,
Your eyes, your personality—you.

The One You Love

The one you love
Doesn't love you anymore.
The feeling
Breaks your heart.

Your heart shatters
Into a million pieces
And you try to pick those
Pieces back up.

Your pieces just sit
In that space until
You can mend them
Back together.

And someone comes
Along, and they mends your
Shattered heart so you can
Live and love again.

Live and love, but
Love always crushes
Your heart until
You find that one person,

And they will never
Break your
Beautiful heart.

The one you love
Always loves you.
The feeling melts
Into your heart.

A Christian

I'm not just average;
I'm not the average person
Or a statistic you use to refer to
People like you.

I am above that.
I don't live under
Your definition
Of a person.

I am not a number:
Not the numbers 1–10
That you count upon
Your hands.

I am not a word
You speak from
Your mouth.

I am not the flesh
That causes you to sin
Or eyes that
Absorb sin into your soul.

I am a man,
A human being
That holds God
Close to my heart.

And by that,
I am not average;
I am above that.
I am holy.

Understand

Just understand
That I am a person,
Not an animal.

Understand
I don't consider the
People that talk
Behind my back, friends.

Understand
I live my life to set myself free,
Not to free others from their
Heavy bondage.

Understand
I'm not one to stand in
The shadows behind someone who thinks they're leading me
In the right direction.

Understand
I'm not a mat
That people walk on day and night
Or wipe their dirt on time and time again.

Understand
I have power that can
Change the minds of people
That can change the minds of this world.

Understand
I have knowledge,
Knowledge that makes a difference.

Understand
Who I am.

Will It?

I can't do it;
I can't be near you.
It sounds mean, but
I can't.

Why?
Is a question that you
Might ask, but I don't
Know if I could tell you.

I think I can try.

I'm scared and afraid;
Every time
You're near
Me, my heart stops.

I don't know what
May come out of my
Mouth, and I'm terrified
Of what I might do.

And, as it kills me to say it,
I like you, and I don't think you'll
Look at me the same way after I tell you.

But I can't hide how I feel;
I'll leave you alone after
I say this.

My heart cries out in a loud voice.
Will it be heard?

Falling for You

Why did I have
To fall for you,
Knowing it would
Never work out?

Why did I
Have to fall for
Those eyes; those
Mesmerizing, beautiful eyes?

Why did I have to fall for
Your smile,
That genuine smile
That made me smile?

Why did I have
To fall flat on
My face for you?

Why, whenever I
Think about you,
My heart beats louder,
And then it
Falls into my feet.

Why do I
Like you?
Why do I think
I love you?

I don't know.

I just want to hold you,
Kiss your bittersweet lips,
And hold your warm hand in mine.

Why did I have to fall for you?

Sure of Love

You came
Into my life,
And when you
Did, my heart grabbed
You.

You came
And changed my world.
I feel for you,
And I think of no one else.

You came
And I saw you,
And my eyes saw
What was inside you.

I saw the
Good in your
Personality.

My heart skipped in my
Chest and jumped into
My throat, and I couldn't
Talk.

It somersaulted
Down into my
Stomach
As you walked away.

You came into my world,
And I love you.

That—I am sure of.

At This Age

At this age,
Love is hard
And even harder
To find.

At this age,
Relationships last
About as long as a
Minute on a clock.

At this age,
Some people
Don't understand
What love is.

At this age,
There are those few
People who understand
How to love.

At this age,
Some people find
The loves of their lives,
And some don't.

At this age,
We really
Don't
Understand.

Tough Break

When things get tough,
They grow even worse,
And you still walk with
Your head held high.

But you're hurting
Inside, and you
Just need someone
To talk to.

Or maybe a hug—
Like a mother holds
Her child when she's
Hurt inside or out.

And if you need
To cry, go ahead.
I will not judge you.
I have my moments, too.

But in the end,
We are still a family.
We are still friends.
I, for one, still love you.

I love you through good times
And bad.

Love Is

Love is
A forbidden dream
That everyone holds close
To aching hearts.

Love is so
Beautiful and hopeful
That the mere thought
Of one loving us is gold.

Love is just
As precious as a child's
Heart, whether the child's heart is
Wounded or not.

Love is rare
And just as hard to find
As if it were hiding in a desert,
Burrowed beneath the sand.

Love is warm
Like a summer night,
When a warm breeze
Feels just right.

Love is hurt,
And it breaks your
Heart over and over,
But it heals you again.

Love is power
In my words
And in my voice.

Love is.

I Love You

My heart
Stopped when
I looked in your
Eyes.

My heart
Caught itself
When you looked
Back at me.

My soul stopped
At the sight of this beautiful
Creation standing before me.

My soul caught
Itself when you
Knew I was there,
In front of you.

My body stopped
When you grabbed
My hand.

My body caught
Itself when I almost
Kissed you.

My mind stopped
Thinking
When I looked at you.

My mind caught
Itself when it accidently
Said
I love you.

Reflections

Reflections

Reflections

Reflections

Reflections

Reflections

Reflections

Reflections

Reflections

Reflections

Reflections

Reflections

Reflections

Reflections

Reflections

Reflections

Reflections

Reflections

Reflections

Reflections
